Jacob H. Hall

Crowning Day

A Collection of gospel songs for Sunday schools, revivals, young people's

meetings, etc. - Vol. 2

Jacob H. Hall

Crowning Day
A Collection of gospel songs for Sunday schools, revivals, young people's meetings, etc. - Vol. 2

ISBN/EAN: 9783337181512

Printed in Europe, USA, Canada, Australia, Japan

Cover: Foto ©Lupo / pixelio.de

More available books at **www.hansebooks.com**

Crowning Day, No. 2

A COLLECTION OF

Gospel Songs

...FOR...

Sunday Schools, Revivals, Young People's Meetings, Etc.

...BY...

J. H. HALL,   J. H. RUEBUSH
and A. S. KIEFFER

Associate Authors:
E. T. Hildebrand, W. H. Ruebush, and J. D. Vaughan

Price, 30 Cents per Copy. $3.00 per Dozen

PREFACE.

May the Beautiful Gospel Songs of "Crowning Day, No. 2," be accompanied by the Holy Spirit and do even more effectual work than those of No. 1.

We send this volume of songs forth to "Sing its own praise," and earnestly hope that it will prove a Messenger of Joy and Peace to many dear hearts wherever it goes.

Yours for Sacred Song,
The Authors.

Copyright, April 1st, 1896, by THE RUEBUSH-KIEFFER Co.

THE CROWNING DAY
No. 2.

"When the chief Shepherd shall appear, ye shall receive a crown of glory that fadeth not away."—1 PETER 5: 4.

No. 131.   **Crown After Cross.**

"Sorrow and sighing shall flee away."—ISA. 35: 10.

Chorus by Rev. J. B. Matthias.   J. H. Hall.

1. How sweet will be the wel-come home When this short life is o'er,
2. When we that bright and heav'n-ly land, With spir-it eyes shall see,
3. O may we live while here be-low, In view of that blest day,
4. When we shall walk the gold-en streets, In gar-ments white and pure;

When pain and sor-row, care and grief, Shall dwell with us no more.
And join the ho-ly an-gel band, In praise, dear Lord of Thee.
When God's bright an-gels shall come down, To bear our souls a-way.
And sing an end-less song of Him Who made our souls se-cure.

CHORUS.

Then palms of vic-to-ry, crowns of glo-ry, Palms of vic-to-ry we shall wear.

Copyright, 1896, by J. H. Hall.

No. 132. There's a Mighty Army Marching.

(This song is respectfully dedicated to the noble army of S. S. workers of W. Va.)

Ida L. Reed.   J. H. Ruebush.

1. There's a might-y ar-my marching; Marshalled by the Prince of Peace,
2. Num-ber-less is this great ar-my, And its ranks are strong and brave,
3. Bless-ed is this might-y ar-my, Meas-ureless the good they do,

O'er them float love's shining banners, Day by day their ranks increase,
And they strive to lead to Je-sus, All the world that He may save.
Toil-ing for the Heav'nly kingdom, To their Lead-er, loy-al, true,

They are march-ing, they are marching, Lift-ing up a-long the way,
They are march-ing, they are marching, Ma-ny are the souls they bring,
They are march-ing, they are marching, On-ward, up-ward ev-er-more,

Sin-ful souls, the weak and fal-len, Win-ning back the steps a-stray.
Won from sin's dark paths and pleasures, Un-to Christ their Prince and King.
Lead-ing mul-ti-tudes of saved ones, To the bright e-ter-nal shore.

Copyright, 1895, by The Ruebush-Kieffer Co.

There's a Mighty Army Marching. Concluded.

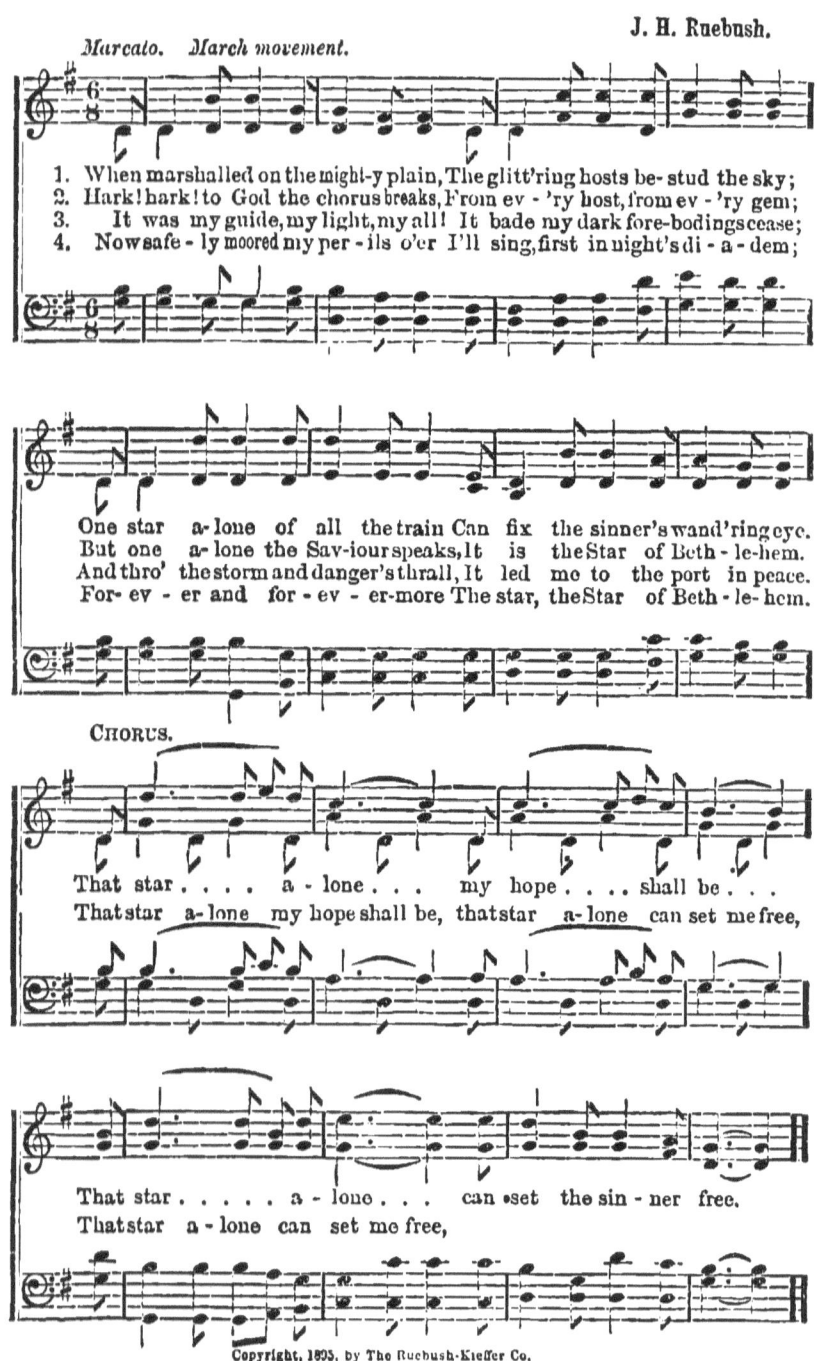

No. 140. The Story Sweet and Old.

Rev. Wm. Houghton.   W. H. Ruebush.

1. Have you listened to the sto-ry sweet and old, Filling life with light and glo-ry men have told, How there came a heav'n-ly stranger, Cra-dle low in Beth'lem's manger, Strong to shield you from all danger, God's dear fold.

2. It is full of human sweetness ev-er new, Rich in love divine completeness, oh, how true! Grief her lone-ly vig-il keeping, Care her trust with sorrow steeping, Lift your eyes and hear it weeping, 'Tis for you.

3. When I heard the wondrous story so di-vine, Coming down thro' annals hoa-ry, Christ was mine, Oh, that love be-yond com-par-ing, Burdened heart thy sorrow bearing, For thy sake the thorn crown wearing, Is he thine?

CHORUS.
{ Oh, the sto - - - - - ry, wondrous sto - ry,
{ Oh, the sto - - - - - ry, sweet old sto - ry,
Sto-ry, sweet old sto-ry, wondrous sto-ry, sweet old sto-ry,
Filling earth with light and glo-ry, glory, light and glory, Tell it o'er and o'er a-gain.

Copyright, 1895, by The Ruebush-Kieffer Co.

No. 142. **What are you Recording?**
W. H. R.   W. H. Ruebush.

1. What are you writ-ing, broth-er? On that page so white and fair,
2. How are you walk-ing, broth-er? In this world so full of care,
3. Oh speak with care, my broth-er, For your words are written there,

Your sins though few, are many Are all re-cord-ed there,
Are you in the path of du-ty? Would you mer-it "well done" there?
Your ev-il thoughts and sayings, Will soil that page so fair.

Just stop and think, my broth-er, Of what you're writing there,
Just step with care, my broth-er, For sinkholes here and there,
Just wait a-while, my broth-er, When words unbridled spring,

FINE.

Are you making on-ly blotches, When the page should be so fair.
And dang'rous places ma-ny, Are 'round you ev-'ry-where.
Just think of pain and suffering, Such words may of-ten bring.

D.S.—For all your deeds and ac-tions, Will face you in "That day."

CHORUS   D.S.

Be care-ful then, my broth-er, Of what you think or say,

Copyright, 1896, by W. H. Ruebush.

No. 144. "Marching Orders."

Wm. H. Gardner.   Wm. A. Ogden.

1. We are sold-iers of the Mas-ter, Ev-er read-y sword in hand;
2. In the night may come the summons, But we mur-mur not a word;
3. Tho' but death there lies be-fore us, Bravely still we take our way;

Wait-ing for our marching or-ders, To be sent on ser-vice grand.
We o-bey our marching or-ders, For the sake of Christ, our Lord.
If He gives the marching or-ders, We will glad-ly all o-bey.

CHORUS.

Waiting for our marching or-ders, Read-y when the word is given,

Proud-ly then we hast-en for-ward For the mighty King of heaven.

Copyright, 1896, by The Ruebush-Kieffer Co.

No. 149. Don't You Want to be Ready?

"Therefore be ye also ready."—Matt. 24 : 44.

Words and Music by F. L. Eiland.

1. Oh! there is a time when the message will come, Don't you want to be ready to go? Oh! sinner the Saviour invites you to-day, Will you hear and make ready to go?
2. To-day is the day of salvation for all, Can you say you are ready to go? A home and a crown is awaiting for thee, Will you come and be ready to go?
3. Oh! yes there's a time when the message will come, Are you willing and ready to go? This moment the Saviour is pleading for thee, Sinner, say, are you ready to go?

Chorus.

Read - - - y to go, Read - - - y to go, Don't you want to be ready to go?
Watching and waiting and ready to go, Don't you want to be waiting and ready to go, yes ready to go.

Copyright, 1896, by F. L. Eiland. From "The Dawning Light," by per.

Don't You Want to be Ready? Concluded.

go?..... Don't you want to be read-y to go?
Read - y to go?

No. 150. My Faith Looks up to Thee.

Dr. Lowell Mason.

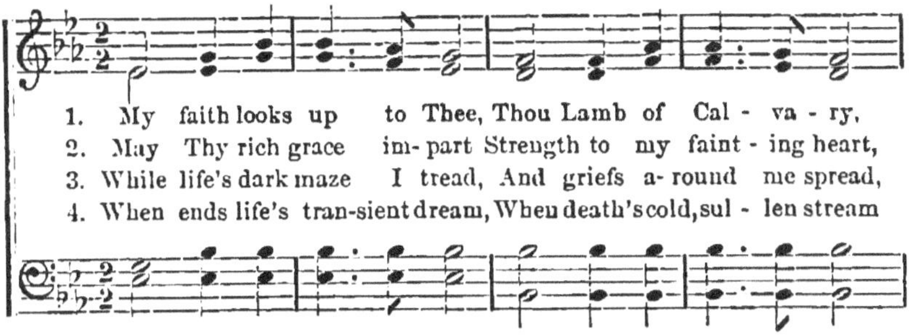

1. My faith looks up to Thee, Thou Lamb of Cal-va-ry,
2. May Thy rich grace im-part Strength to my faint-ing heart,
3. While life's dark maze I tread, And griefs a-round me spread,
4. When ends life's tran-sient dream, When death's cold, sul-len stream

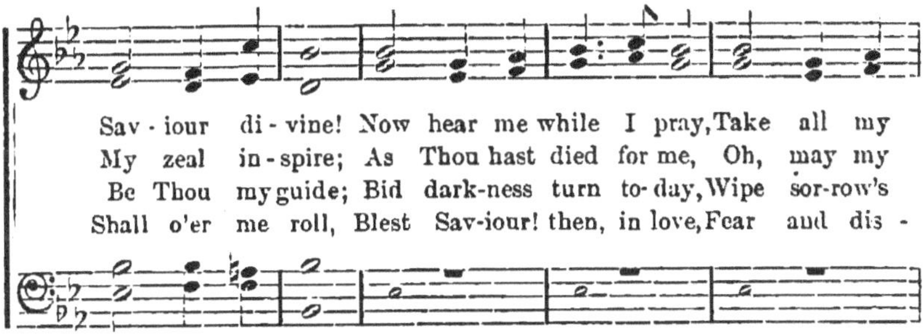

Sav-iour di-vine! Now hear me while I pray, Take all my
My zeal in-spire; As Thou hast died for me, Oh, may my
Be Thou my guide; Bid dark-ness turn to-day, Wipe sor-row's
Shall o'er me roll, Blest Sav-iour! then, in love, Fear and dis-

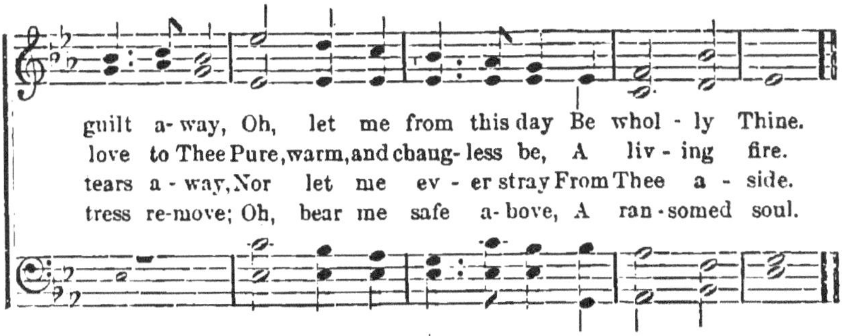

guilt a-way, Oh, let me from this day Be whol-ly Thine.
love to Thee Pure, warm, and chang-less be, A liv-ing fire.
tears a-way, Nor let me ev-er stray From Thee a-side.
tress re-move; Oh, bear me safe a-bove, A ran-somed soul.

No. 151. Victory O'er the Grave.

Laura E. Newell
J. H. Hall.

1. Grave where is thy vic-'try? Death where is thy sting? Jesus rose in tri-umph! glory to the King! Sound the bless-ed tid-ings! Jesus lives a-gain! Death for-ev-er vanquished! shout the glad re-frain!
2. Jesus died in an-guish on the cru-el tree! But He rose Ho-san-na! brings us lib-er-ty! Vic-tor! King su-per-nal! glo-ri-ous in might, Jesus brings His people ev-er-last-ing light.
3. Glo-ry in the high-est! shout the grand re-frain Bear a-broad the mes-sage, Jesus lives a-gain! Heav'n and earth in cho-rus, join in songs of praise, Un-to our Re-deem-er hearts and voi-ces raise.
4. Jesus on-ly Jesus, still our song shall be, Jesus loves His peo-ple, He doth set us free, Nev-er-more in bond-age sin can us en-thrall, Christ our blest re-demp-tion, hath reclaimed us all.

Chorus.

Glo-ry be to God! Jesus lives! Jesus lives! He'll redeem the lost!

Copyright, 1896, by J. H. Hall.

Victory O'er the Grave. Concluded.

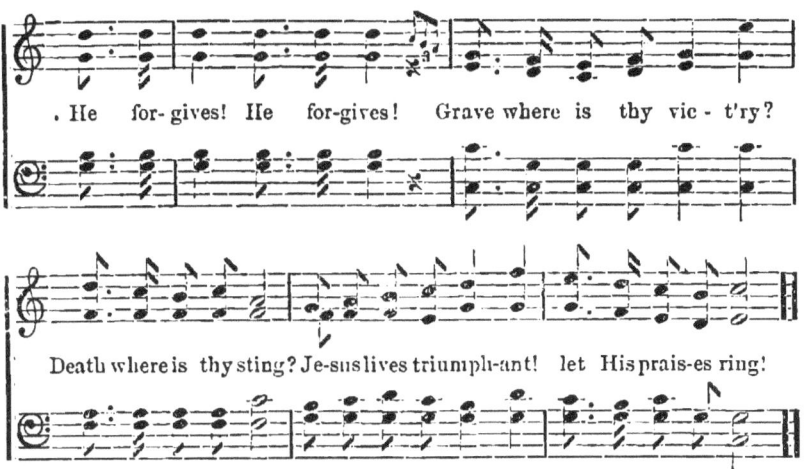

. He for-gives! He for-gives! Grave where is thy vic - t'ry?

Death where is thy sting? Jesus lives triumph-ant! let His prais-es ring!

No. 152. Come, Ye that Love the Lord.

Rev. Isaac Watts.   Rev. C. R. Dunbar.

1. Come, ye that love the Lord, And let your joys be known;
2. Let those re - fuse to sing Who nev - er knew our God;
3. The hill of Zi - on yields A thou-sand sa - cred sweets,
4. There we shall see His face, And nev - er, nev - er sin;
5. Then let our songs a - bound, And ev - 'ry tear be dry;

Cho.—I'm glad sal - va - tion's free, I'm glad sal - va - tion's free;

Join in a song with sweet ac-cord, While ye surround the throne.
But chil-dren of the heav'n-ly King May speak their joys a-broad.
Be - fore we reach the heav'n-ly fields, Or walk the Gold-en Streets.
There, from the riv - ers of His grace, Drink end-less pleasures in.
We're marching thro' Im-man-uel's ground To fair - er worlds on high.

Sal - va - tion's free for you and me; I'm glad sal - vation's free.

We Are Marching On. Concluded.

from each eye, March-ing on, March-ing on.
march-ing on,

No. 154.   **Land of Promise.**

Isaac Watts.   Arr. from Rink by G. F. Root.

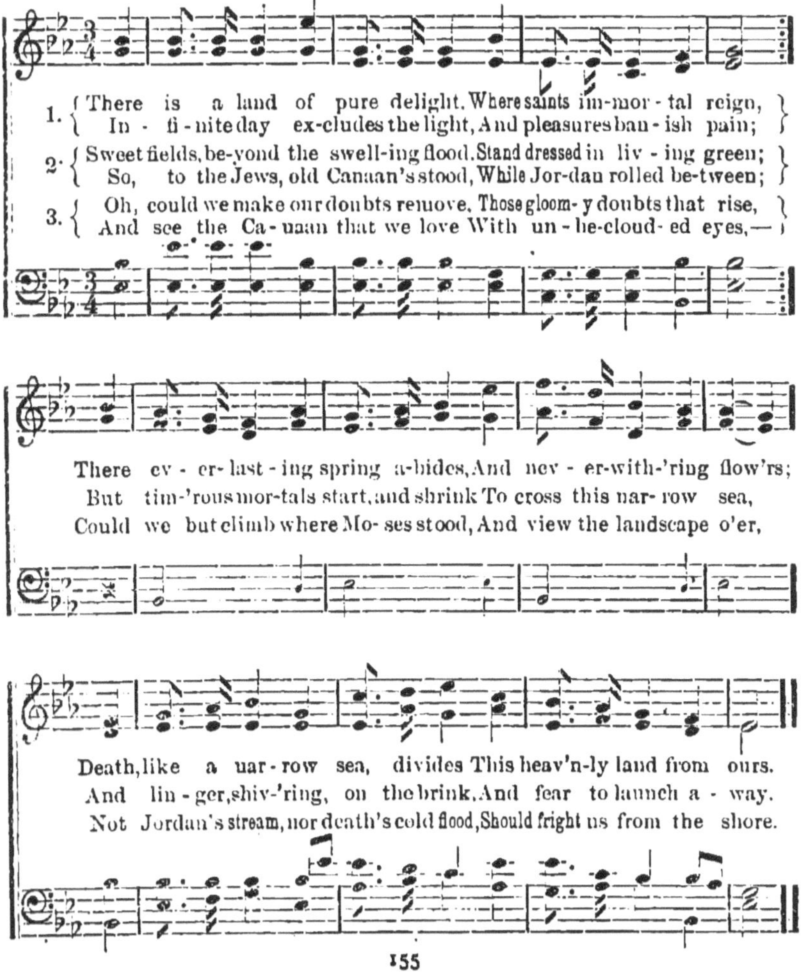

1. { There is a land of pure delight, Where saints im-mor-tal reign,
    { In-fi-nite day ex-cludes the light, And pleasures ban-ish pain;
2. { Sweet fields, be-yond the swell-ing flood, Stand dressed in liv-ing green;
    { So, to the Jews, old Canaan's stood, While Jor-dan rolled be-tween;
3. { Oh, could we make our doubts remove, Those gloom-y doubts that rise,
    { And see the Ca-naan that we love With un-be-cloud-ed eyes,—

There ev-er-last-ing spring a-bides, And nev-er-with-'ring flow'rs;
But tim-'rous mor-tals start, and shrink To cross this nar-row sea,
Could we but climb where Mo-ses stood, And view the landscape o'er,

Death, like a nar-row sea, divides This heav'n-ly land from ours.
And lin-ger, shiv-'ring, on the brink, And fear to launch a-way.
Not Jordan's stream, nor death's cold flood, Should fright us from the shore.

Ho! Every One That Thirsteth. Concluded.

drink,   Drink the   life that com-eth from a-bove.
Come and drink,

No. 162.   **The Happy Day.**

Rev. Philip Doddridge.   Edward F. Rimbault.

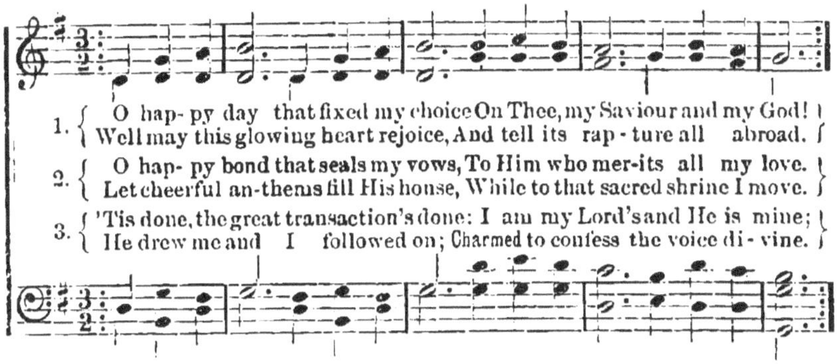

1. { O hap-py day that fixed my choice On Thee, my Saviour and my God!
   { Well may this glowing heart rejoice, And tell its rap-ture all abroad.
2. { O hap-py bond that seals my vows, To Him who mer-its all my love.
   { Let cheerful an-thems fill His house, While to that sacred shrine I move.
3. { 'Tis done, the great transaction's done: I am my Lord's and He is mine;
   { He drew me and I followed on; Charmed to confess the voice di-vine.

Refrain.   FINE.

Hap-py day, hap-py day, When Je-sus washed my sins a-way.

D.S.

He taught me how to watch and pray, And live re-joic-ing ev-'ry day.

4 Now rest my long-divided heart,
  Fixed on this blissful center, rest;
Nor ever from thy Lord depart,
  With Him of every good posessed.

5 High heaven that heard the solemn vow,
  That vow renewed shall daily hear,
Till in life's latest hour I bow,
  And bless in death a bond so dear.

No. 165. Seeking a Refuge.

"God is our refuge and strength, a very present help in time of trouble.—Psa. 46: 1."

L. A. M. Rev. L. A. Morris.

1. Near-er my Sav-iour, still near-er to Thee, This earth's fleeting com-forts, are noth-ing to me; Per-ish-ing dai-ly, like shad-ows they flee, I'm seek-ing a ref-uge, blest Sav-iour in Thee.
2. Though I have wandered a-gain and a-gain, Yet ev-er I hear this in-vit-ing re-frain; Let noth-ing keep thee a-way from my love, It turns my af-fections to heav-en a-bove.
3. Dark are the shad-ows of sor-row and woe, But Je-sus will light up the path-way I know; Beau-ti-ful man-sions a-wait-ing on high, With this blest as-surance, my hope can-not die.
4. When the dark val-ley I'm called to pass thro', A light from those mansions will o-pen to view; Je-sus, my Sav-iour, the bright Morning Star, Will lead to the cit-y whose gates are a-jar.

Chorus.

Seek-ing a ref-uge, seek-ing a ref-uge, I'm seek-ing a ref-uge, blest Sav-iour in Thee. Seek-ing a ref-uge,

Copyright, 1895, by The Ruebush-Kieffer Co.

Seeking a Refuge. Concluded.

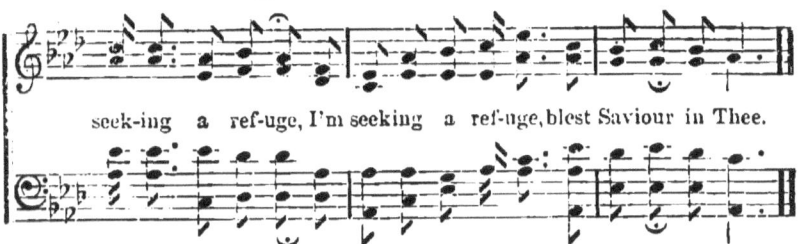

No. 166. When Thou Comest.

"Lord, remember me when thou comest into thy kingdom."—LUKE 13 : 42.

W. A. O.   W. A. Ogden.

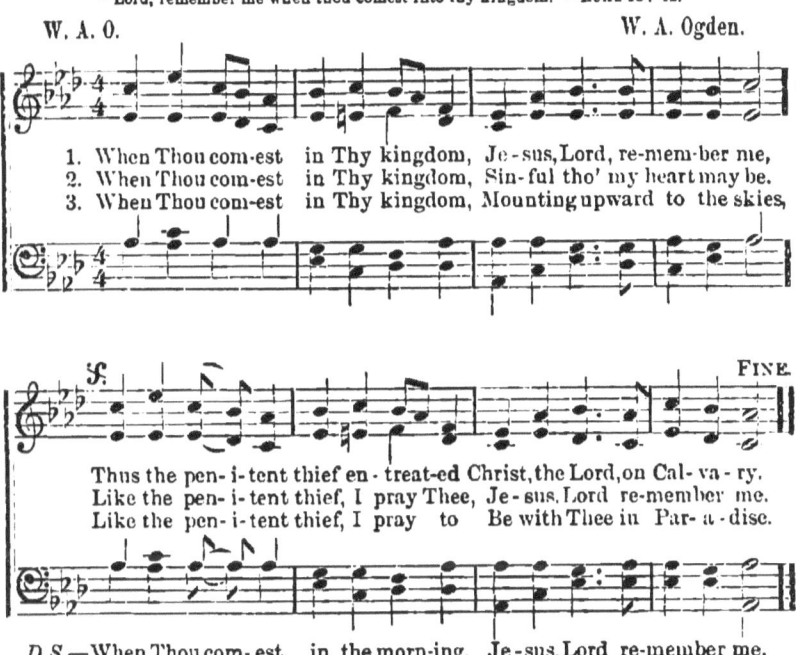

1. When Thou com-est in Thy kingdom, Je-sus, Lord, re-mem-ber me,
2. When Thou com-est in Thy kingdom, Sin-ful tho' my heart may be.
3. When Thou com-est in Thy kingdom, Mounting upward to the skies,

Thus the pen-i-tent thief en-treat-ed Christ, the Lord, on Cal-va-ry.
Like the pen-i-tent thief, I pray Thee, Je-sus, Lord re-mem-ber me.
Like the pen-i-tent thief, I pray to Be with Thee in Par-a-dise.

D. S.—When Thou com-est in the morn-ing, Je-sus, Lord re-mem-ber me.

Chorus.

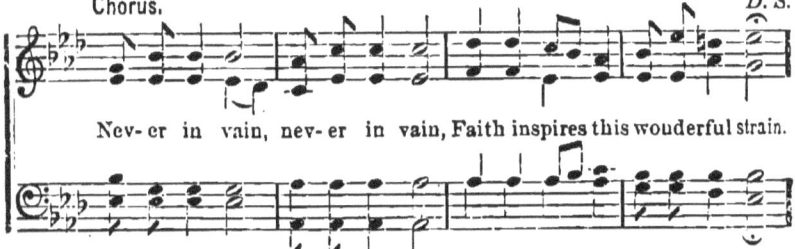

Nev-er in vain, nev-er in vain, Faith inspires this wonderful strain.

By permission of W. A. Ogden, owner of the copyright.

No. 169. Lead Me Gently Home, Father.

3 Lo! I will be with you alway,
  I will never forsake,
Saith the Lord, till in my likeness,
  Ye with joy shall awake.
Where the tree of life is vernal,
  Ever blooming and fair,
And where songs of praise eternal,
  Float on heaven's balmy air.

4 I am waiting, I am longing,
  For the bright, golden day,
When His blessed voice shall call me,
  To that land far away.
And while here He bids me tarry,
  Let me toil as I roam,
Till beyond the clouds and sorrows,
  I shall praise Him at home.

Copyright, 1896, by J. H. Hall.

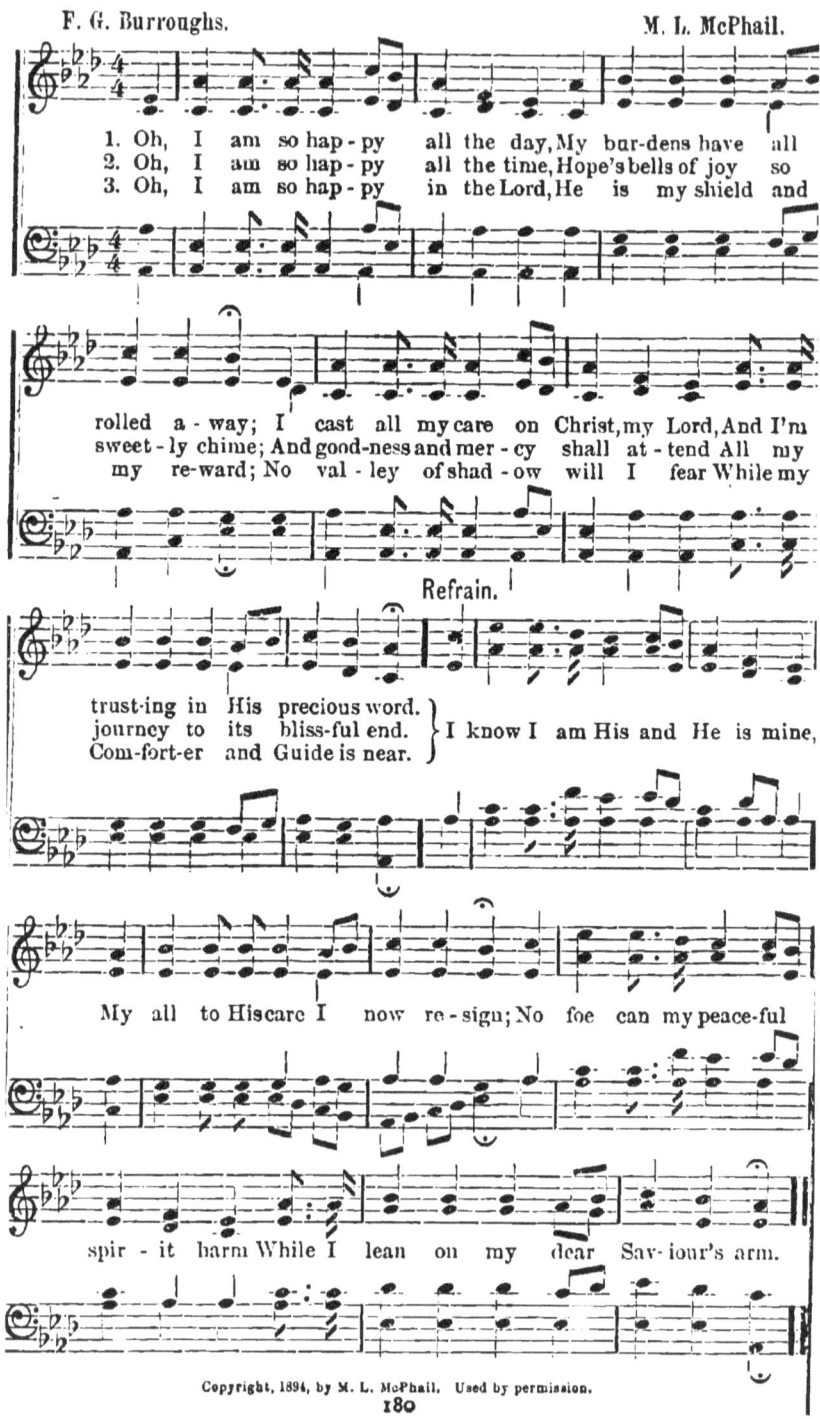

I Want to Live for Jesus. Concluded.

I want to go to Jesus, And forever be at home.

No. 186. Beneath His Wing.

Edwin H. Nevins, D.D.   J. H. Fillmore.

1. Beneath His wing I sweetly rest, While balmy peace reigns in my breast;
2. Amidst all dangers, seen or known, His guardian wing is o'er me thrown;
3. This heav'nly wing, so widely spread, Is over me where'er I tread;
4. When wasting on the bed of death, I still can sing with dying breath,

I never need a foe to dread, While His bright wing is o'er me spread.
It soothes me with its magic power, And turns to light the darkest hour.
It banishes all gloom and fear To feel assured His wing is near.
For round me I can clearly see Christ's wing of love o'er-arching me.

Refrain.   *repeat slowly.*

Beneath His wing, beneath His wing.
Beneath His wing my heart doth sing, beneath, beneath His wing.

Copyright, 1890, by Fillmore Bros. Used by per.

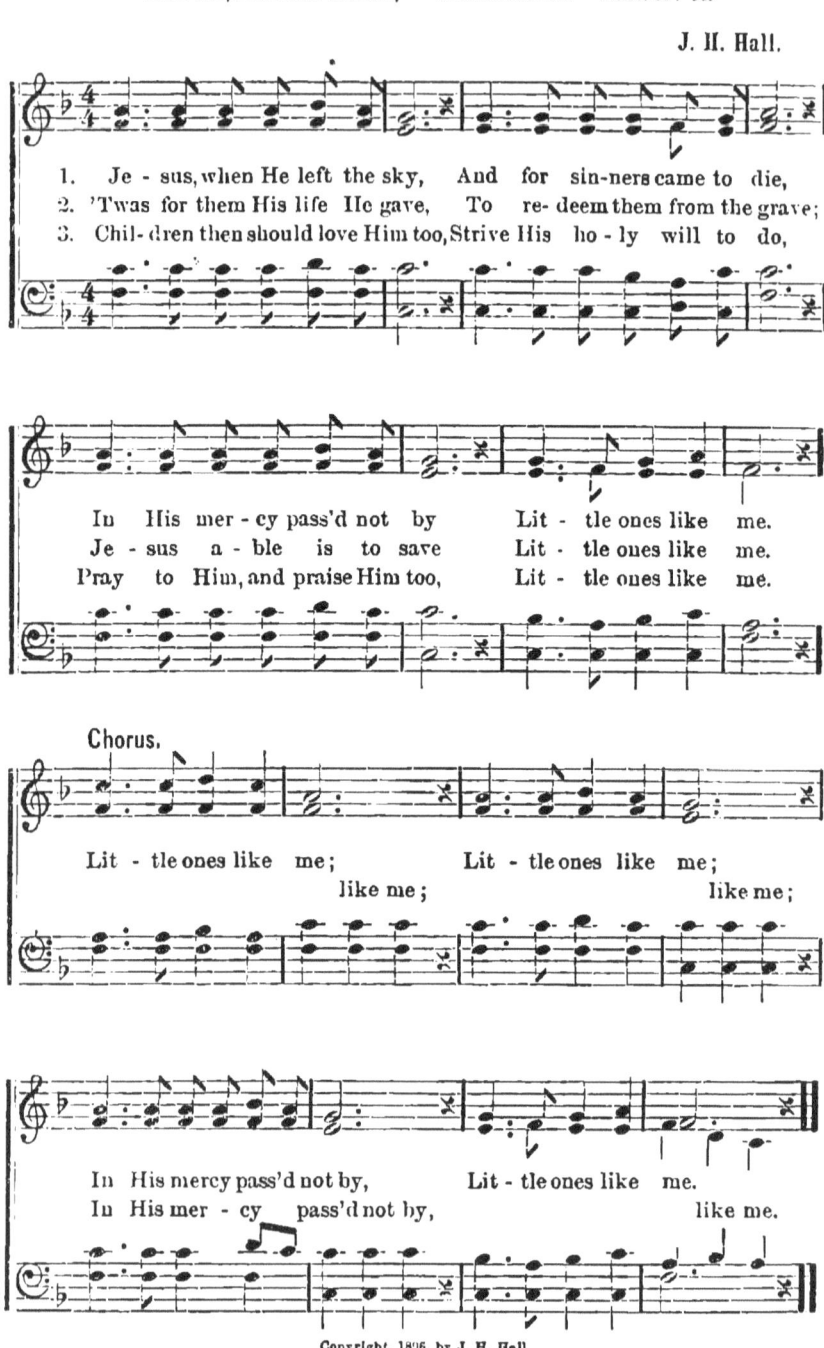

No. 192. Footsteps of Jesus.

Mrs. M. B. C. Slade.   Dr. A. B. Everett.

1. Sweet-ly, Lord, have we heard thee call-ing, Come, fol-low me!
2. Tho' they lead o'er the cold dark mountains, Seek-ing His sheep;
3. If they lead thro' the tem-ple ho-ly, Preach-ing the word;
4. By and by, thro' the shin-ing por-tals, Turn-ing our feet,
5. Then at last when on high He sees us, Our jour-ney done,

And we see where thy foot-prints fall-ing, Lead us to thee.
Or a-long by Si-lo-am's fount-ains, Help-ing the weak.
Or in homes of the poor and low-ly, Serv-ing the Lord.
We shall walk, with the glad im-mor-tals, Heav'n's golden street.
We will rest where the steps of Je-sus, End at His throne.

Chorus.

Foot-prints of Je-sus, that make the path-way glow;

We will fol-low the steps of Je-sus, Wher-e'er they go.

Used by permission of The R. M. McIntosh Co., Atlanta, Ga., owners of the copyright.

Lead Me to the Rock. Concluded.

Rock, To the Rock that is high-er than I.
Lead me to the Rock,

No. 194. Come, Sinner, Come.

Will. E. Witter. Dr. H. R. Palmer.

1. While Je-sus whispers to you, Come, sin-ner, come! While we are
2. Are you too heav-y la-den? Come, sin-ner, come! Je-sus will
3. Oh, hear His ten-der pleading, Come, sin-ner, come! Come and re-

pray-ing for you, Come, sin-ner, come! Now is the time to own Him,
bear your burden, Come, sin-ner, come! Je-sus will not deceive you,
ceive the bless-ing, Come, sin-ner, come! While Je-sus whispers to you,

Come, sin-ner, come! Now is the time to know Him, Come, sinner, come!
Come, sin-ner, come! Je-sus can now redeem you, Come, sinner, come!
Come, sin-ner, come! While we are praying for you, Come, sinner, come!

Used by permission of Dr. H. R. Palmer, owner of copyright.

No. 197. I Love to Tell the Story.

"I will speak of Thy wondrous work."

Miss Kate Hankey, 1867.   W. G. Fischer, by per.

1. I love to tell the Story Of unseen things above, Of Jesus and His Glory, Of Jesus and His love! I love to tell the Story! Because I know its true; It satisfies my longings, As nothing else would do.

2. I love to tell the Story! More wonderful it seems, Than all the golden fancies Of all our golden dreams. I love to tell the Story! It did so much for me! And that is just the reason, I tell it now to thee.

3. I love to tell the Story! 'Tis pleasant to repeat It seems, each time I tell it, More wonderfully sweet. I love to tell the Story! For some have never heard The message of salvation From God's own Holy word.

4. I love to tell the Story! For those who know it best Seem hungering and thirsting To hear it, like the rest. And when, in scenes of glory, I sing the New, New Song, 'Twill be the Old, Old Story That I have loved so long.

Chorus.

I love to tell the Story! 'Twill be my theme in glory, To tell the Old, Old Story Of Jesus and His love.

No. 199. A Work for All.

"Go work to-day in my vineyard."—MATT. 21:28.

Laura E. Newell.   J. H. Hall.

1. There's a work, a work that we all may do, For our
2. There's a work, a work and it must be done, If we
3. There's a cross, a cross for us each to bear, But His

Sav-iour if we will, Then with joy, with joy let's our task pur-sue.
live and strive a-right, With the end in view, blest the work begun,
strength each day He'll give, And at last a crown we in heav'n may wear,

Chorus.

And our miss-ion here ful-fill.
Let us la-bor with our might.
Near to Je-sus let us live.

There's a work that each may do for Je-sus, We may serve Him ev-'ry day, (yes,) We may tell His love to those who wander, We may seek the lambs a-stray.

Copyright, 1896, by J. H. Hall.

No. 200. The Beautiful Golden Gate.

Edwin Oliver. Arr. by O. E. Murray.

1. There is a gate that o-pens wide, The beau-ti-ful gold-en gate,
2. Do you de-sire to en-ter thro' The beau-ti-ful gold-en gate?
3. Pre-pare, for soon the time will come, To en-ter that gold-en gate,
4. How sad the words "too late, too late" To en-ter the gold-en gate!
5. O would you walk the streets of gold, Then en-ter the gold-en gate,

'Twas o-pened when the Sav-iour died, The beau-ti-ful gold-en gate.
Re-pent, or you will nev-er view The beau-ti-ful gold-en gate.
Ex-cept ye be con-vert-ed here, None en-ter the gold-en gate.
May they not seal your last es-tate. Come en-ter the gold-en gate.
Would see the glo-ry long fore-told, Then en-ter the gold-en gate.

Chorus.

The beau-ti-ful gold-en gate, Where heav-en-ly an-gels wait,

Repeat Chorus pp.

You may ac-cept the Sav-iour now If you en-ter the gold-en gate.

Used by per. of Rev. E. O. Murray.

Guide Me, Saviour. Concluded.

No. 202. Dear Lord, Remember Me.

Isaac Watts.   Music and Chorus by Asa Hull.

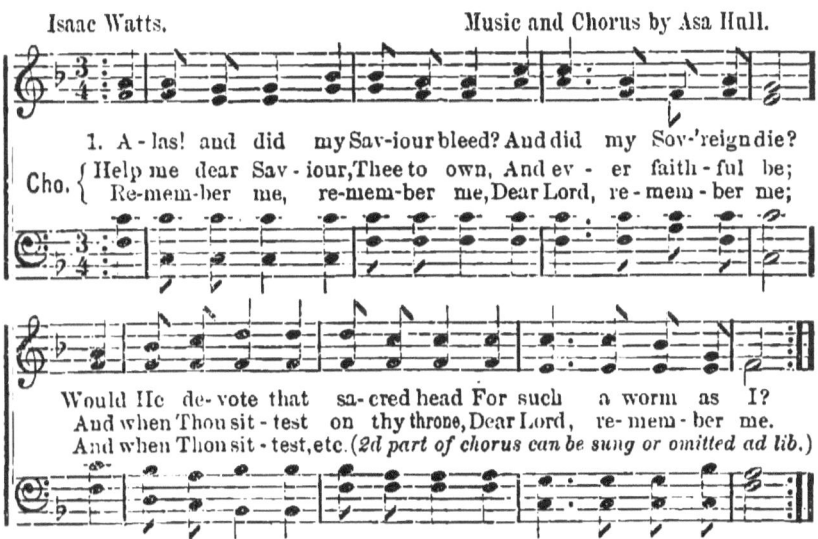

2 Was it for crimes that I have done
   He groaned upon the tree?
   Amazing pity! grace unknown!
   And love beyond degree.

3 Well might the sun in darkness hide,
   And shut His glory in,
   When Christ, the mighty Maker, died
   For man, the creature's, sin.

4 Thus might I hide my blushing face
   While His dear cross appears;
   Dissolve my heart in thankfulness,
   And melt mine eyes to tears.

5 But drops of grief can ne'er repay
   The debt of love I owe;
   Here, Lord, I give myself away,—
   'Tis all that I can do.

Copyright, 1867, by Asa Hull. Re-entered, 1896. By per.

Death is Only a Dream. Concluded.

Chorus.
On-ly a dream, on-ly a dream, And glo-ry beyond the dark stream; How peaceful the slumber, how happy the waking; For death is on-ly a dream.

* Words of Chorus by A. J. Buchanan.

No. 204.   **Turning to God.**

"I would seek unto God."—JOB 5: 8.

D. W. H.   D. W. Henderson.

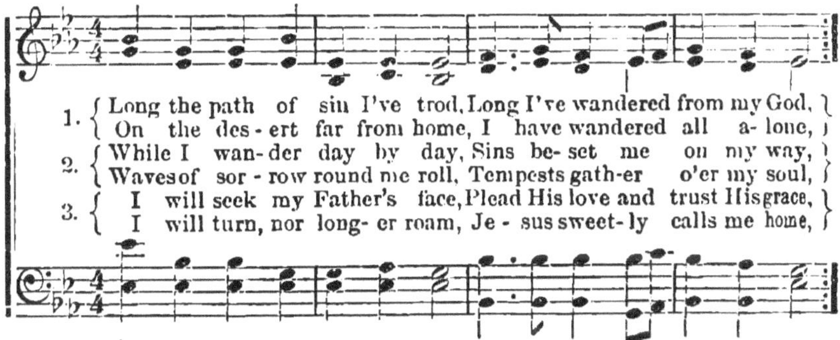

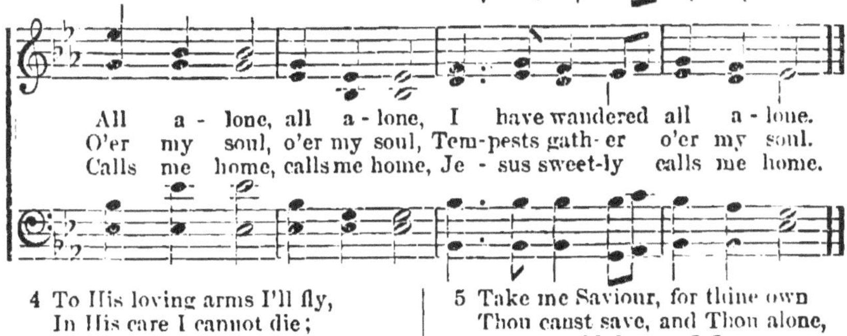

1. Long the path of sin I've trod, Long I've wandered from my God,
On the des-ert far from home, I have wandered all a-lone,
All a-lone, all a-lone, I have wandered all a-lone.

2. While I wan-der day by day, Sins be-set me on my way,
Waves of sor-row round me roll, Tempests gath-er o'er my soul,
O'er my soul, o'er my soul, Tem-pests gath-er o'er my soul.

3. I will seek my Father's face, Plead His love and trust His grace,
I will turn, nor long-er roam, Je-sus sweet-ly calls me home,
Calls me home, calls me home, Je-sus sweet-ly calls me home.

4 To His loving arms I'll fly,
In His care I cannot die;
Saviour Thou who loves me best,
On Thy bosom let me rest,
Let me rest, let me rest,
On Thy bosom let me rest.

5 Take me Saviour, for thine own
Thou canst save, and Thou alone,
From my idols now I flee.
I resign them all for Thee,
All for Thee, all for Thee
I resign them all for Thee.

Copyright, 1896, by J. H. Hall.

In Sight of the Crystal Sea. Concluded.

star - crown'd take their seats, But none could I call my own.
say, "I know you not," How-e'er I may knock and pray.
life, I'd give up the strife, And serve Him for - ev - er - more.
dead?" to my-self I said "An end is there ne'er to be."

5 It seemed as tho' I woke from a dream,
 How sweet was the light of day!
 Melodious sounded the Sabbath bells
 From towers that were far away,
 I then became as a child,
 And I wept afresh;
 For the Lord had taken my heart of stone,
 And given a heart of flesh.

6 Still oft I sit with life's memories,
 And I think of the crystal sea;
 And I see the thrones of star-crown'd ones,
 I know there's a crown for me;
 And when the voice of the Judge says, come,
 Of the Judge on the great white throne,
 I know 'mid the thrones of the star-crown'd
 There's one I shall call my own. [ones,

No. 210. Jesus, Saviour, Pilot Me.

Rev. Edward Hopper, D.D.   J. E. Gould.

1. Je - sus, Sav - iour, pi - lot me, O - ver Life's tem-pestuous sea,
2. As a moth - er stills her child, Thou canst hush the o-cean wild;
3. When at last I near the shore, And the fear - ful breakers roar

Unknown waves a-round me roll, Hid - ing rock and treach'rous shoal,
Boist'rous waves o - bey Thy will, When Thou say-est "peace, be still;"
'Twixt me and my peace-ful rest, Then while lean - ing on Thy breast,

Chart and com - pass come from Thee, Je - sus, Sav - iour, pi - lot me.
Wond'rous sov-'reign of the sea, Je - sus, Sav - iour, pi - lot me.
May I hear Thee say to me, "Fear not, I will pi - lot thee."

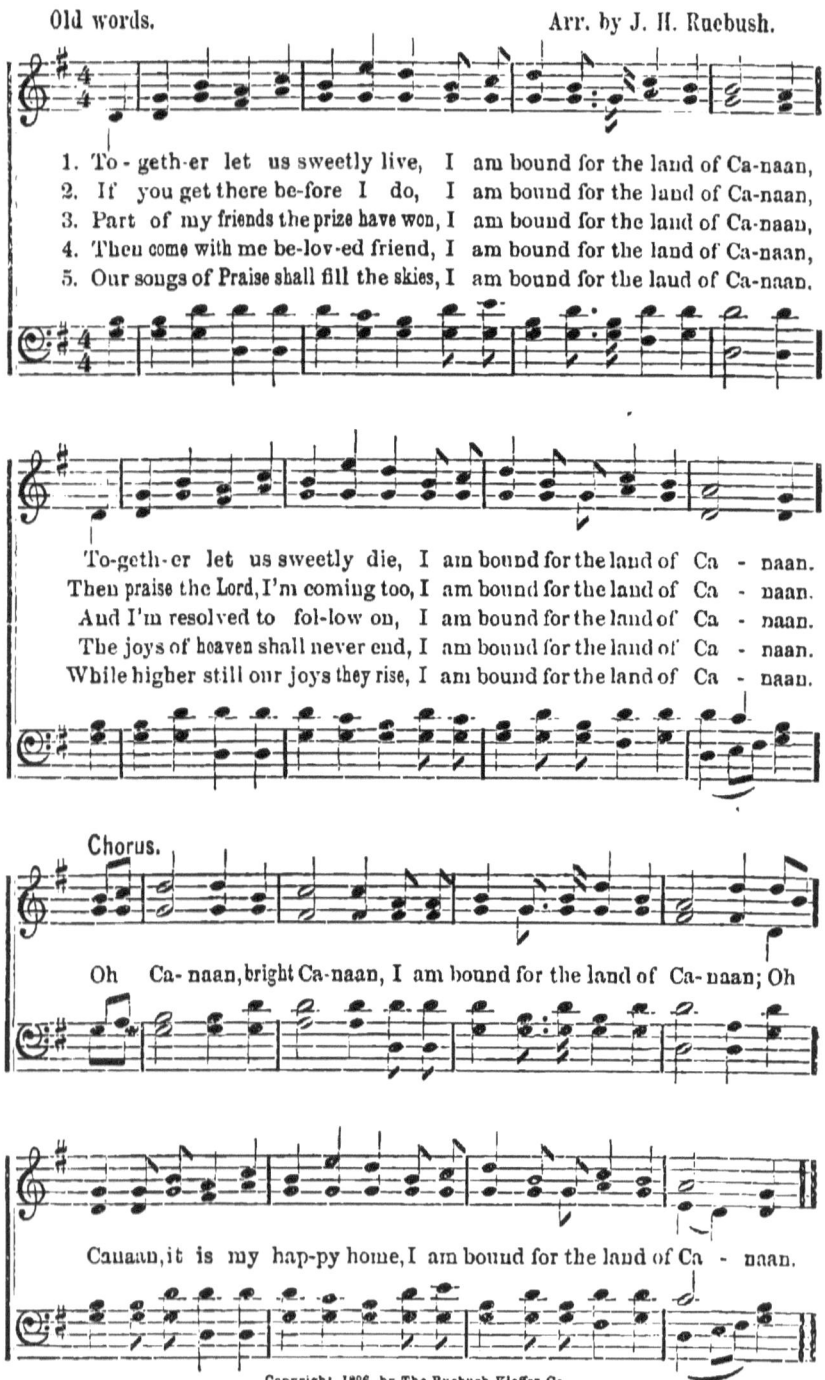

No. 212. Abide With Me.

Rev. J. E. Rankin, D. D. Chas. Edw. Prior.

5 Abide with me.
"My peace be with thee!" this thine evening greeting;
Thus let me see the radiance of Thy face;
How swift to night the day of life is fleeting,
And death and life beyond come on apace.
Abide with me.

6 Abide with me.
Soon will for me these earthly scenes be ending
Like some brief vision of night-watches fled;
The length'ning shadows on life's hills descending,
And the last word above my dust be said.
Abide with me.

7 Abide with me.
Ah, then O Lord, through Thy rich grace I enter
That land of which Thou art the life and light;
Where from all climes Thy ransomed captives enter,
And know no parting, or descending night.
Abide with me.

Copyright, 1896, by C. E. Prior. By per.

Christ, or the World. Concluded.

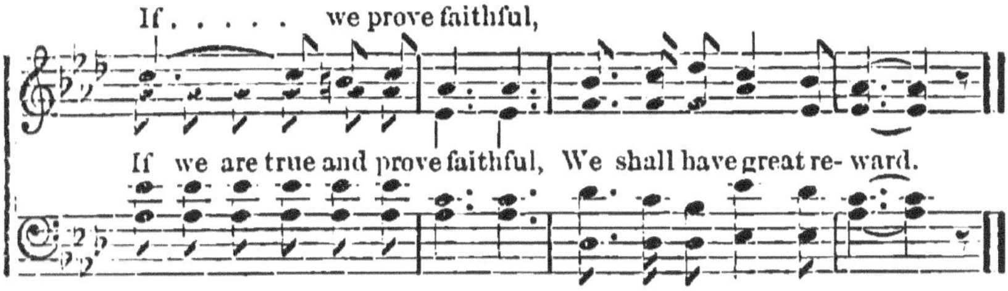

If . . . . we prove faithful,
If we are true and prove faithful, We shall have great reward.

No. 214. Sing Glory!

Rev. Wm. Appel. A. Beirly.

1. My heart is fixed to praise the Lord, Glo-ry, glo-ry, hal-le-lu-jah!
2. The fair-est of the fair is He, Glo-ry, glo-ry, hal-le-lu-jah!
3. I'm still re-joic-ing in His love, Glo-ry, glo-ry, hal-le-lu-jah!
4. In heav'n I'll sing it o'er and o'er, Glo-ry, glo-ry, hal-le-lu-jah!

I'm feed-ing on His pre-cious word, Glo-ry, glo-ry, hal-le-lu-jah!
To see His bless-ed face, will be Glo-ry, glo-ry, hal-le-lu-jah!
I'm go-ing to my home a-bove, Glo-ry, glo-ry, hal-le-lu-jah!
I'll praise the Sav-iour more and more, Glo-ry, glo-ry, hal-le-lu-jah!

Chorus.
The Sav-iour is my faithful Friend! Sing glo-ry, sing glo-ry! I'll sing His prais-es with-out end, Sing glo-ry, glo-ry, hal-le-lu-jah!

Copyright, 1894, by A. Beirly. Used by permission.

No. 218. **The Open Fountain.**

"In that day there shall be a fountain opened.........for sin and uncleanness."—ZECH. 13:1.

J. D. V.   Jas. D. Vaughan.

1. There's a pre-cious fountain o-pened, For un-clean-ness and for sin,
2. Though your sins may be as scar-let, They shall be as white as snow,
3. Oh! my friend why do you lin-ger, Wash in Cal-vary's crimson wave,
4. Will you heed the in-vi-ta-tion, Come to Je-sus, don't de-lay,
5. When your dear-est friends forsake you; In your sor-est want and need,

And the in-vi-ta-tion giv-en, On-ly come and wash there-in.
He who wash-es in this fount-ain Shall its heal-ing vir-tues know.
Come now for there's no re-pent-ance, In the cold and si-lent grave.
Ere to-mor-row death may claim you, Oh, to-day's sal-va-tion's day.
Then the sym-pa-thiz-ing Je-sus, Will be-come a Friend in-deed.

Chorus.

Oh! the pre-cious blood of Je-sus, Fount of cleans-ing, full and free,

Come and wash and live for-ev-er, It was shed for you and me.

No. 220.   Trust in the Lord.

Strive to Follow Jesus. Concluded.

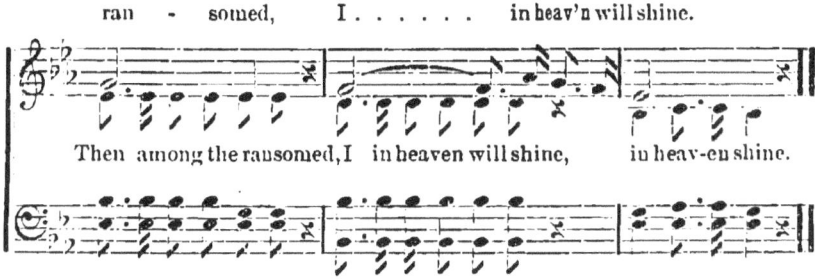

ran - somed, I . . . . . . in heav'n will shine.

Then among the ransomed, I in heaven will shine, in heav-en shine.

No. 222. Fair Haven.

Scotch Air.

Slow.

1. Hail! sweet-est, dear-est tie that binds Our glow-ing hearts is one;
2. No ling-'ring hope, no part - ing sigh, Our fu - ture meeting knows;

FINE.

Hail! sa - cred hope, that tunes our minds To har - mo - ny di - vine;
The friend-ship beams from ev - 'ry eye, And hope im-mor - tal grows:

D.S.—The hope, when days and years have pass'd, We all shall meet in heav'n.

D.S.

It is the hope, the bliss - ful hope Which Je - sus' grace has giv'n;
Oh, sa - cred hope, oh, bliss - ful hope, Which Je - sus' grace has giv'n;

The Wondrous Cross. Concluded.

tempt.... on all my pride,.... My richest gain,....
You pour contempt on all my pride, My richest gain,
I count but loss,... When e'er I view, I view the wondrous cross...
I count but loss, the wondrous cross.

No. 224. **Gratitude.**

Rev. P-A. I-D. Bost

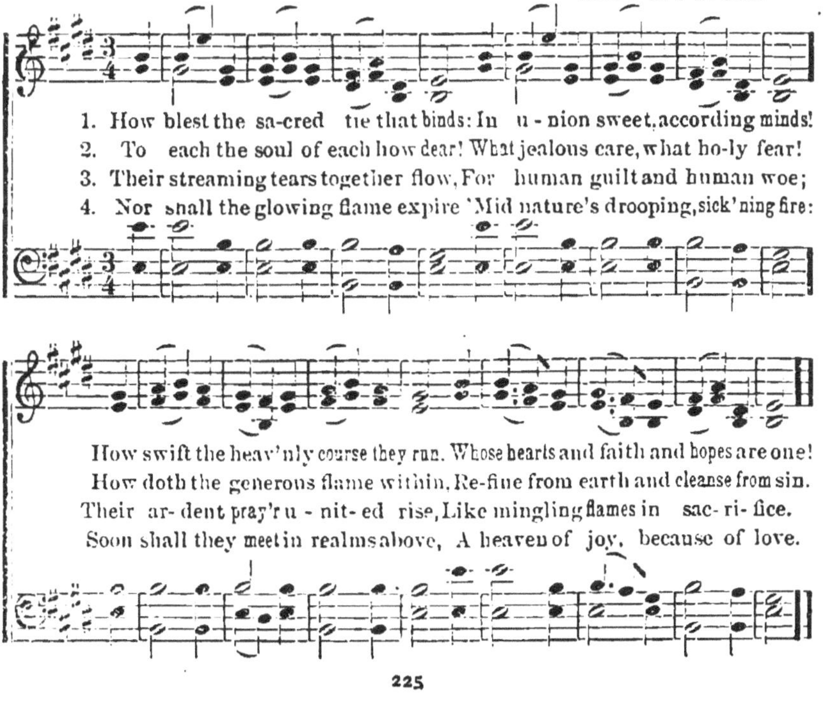

1. How blest the sa-cred tie that binds: In u-nion sweet, according minds!
2. To each the soul of each how dear! What jealous care, what ho-ly fear!
3. Their streaming tears together flow, For human guilt and human woe;
4. Nor shall the glowing flame expire 'Mid nature's drooping, sick'ning fire:

How swift the heav'nly course they run, Whose hearts and faith and hopes are one!
How doth the generous flame within, Re-fine from earth and cleanse from sin.
Their ar-dent pray'r u-nit-ed rise, Like mingling flames in sac-ri-fice.
Soon shall they meet in realms above, A heaven of joy, because of love.

Where the Living Waters Flow. Concluded.

For Je-sus and the right, Down where the living waters flow.
liv-ing waters flow.

No. 226.   Jesus Will Let You In.

A. S. K.   A. S. Kieffer.

1. { Come to our Fa-ther's house, Come, ere the day be gone; }
   { Temp-ests are gath-'ring fast, Dark-ness is com-ing on. }
2. { Look at the wea-ry way, Look where thy feet have trod; }
   { Find-ing no rest nor peace, Wand-'ring a-way from God. }
3. { Dark-er thy path-way grows, Soon will the night come down; }
   { Fierce-ly the light-nings flash, Dark-er the tem-pests frown. }

Fly, for the tempest is com-ing, Sweeping the fields of sin;
Knock at the por-tals of mer-cy, Je-sus will let you in.

4 Fly from the fields of sin,
  Fly for thy life to-day;
  Fly to our Father's house,
  Enter the narrow way.

5 Here will thy soul find rest,
  Safe from each angry blast;
  Here find a perfect peace,—
  Joys that forever last.

The Ruebush-Kieffer Co., owners of Copyright.

No. 228. The Loving Little Ones.

Rev. E. Unangst. Gunture, India.   J. H. Kurzenknabe.

1. 'Tis Je-sus loves the lit-tle ones And calls them as His own;
2. Let lit-tle ones sing Je-sus' name—He loves to hear them sing,—
3. He loves to be with lit-tle ones, And hear their child-like prayer;
4. 'Tis Je-sus whom the lit-tle ones, May call their lov-ing King;

He's al-ways with the lit-tle ones, They're nev-er left a-lone.
And fill His courts with joy-ful sound, And make His prais-es ring.
And ten-der-ly He takes them up In-to His lov-ing arms.
'Tis He that makes them an-gels too, His name for aye too sing.

Chorus.

The lov-ing lit-tle ones, The love-ly lit-tle ones,
The lov-ing, lov-ing lit-tle ones, The love-ly, love-ly lit-tle ones,

The bless-ed lit-tle ones, The hap-py lit-tle ones
The bless-ed, bless-ed lit-tle ones, The hap-py lit-tle ones

Copyright, 1891, by J. H. Kurzenknabe. Used by per.

What Shall Our Answers be? Concluded.

No. 232.   **The Great Physician.**

Rev. Wm. Hunter.   Rev. J. H. Stockton.

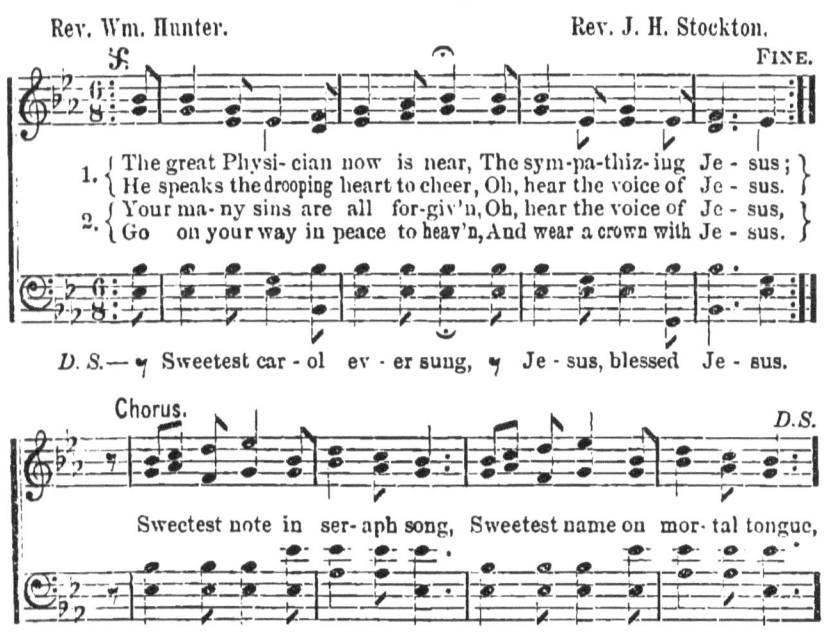

3 All glory to the dying Lamb!
  I now believe in Jesus;
  I love the blessed Saviour's name,
  I love the name of Jesus.

4 His name dispels my guilt, and fear,
  No other name but Jesus;
  Oh! how my soul delights to hear
  The charming name of Jesus.

No. 234. The Flowing Fountain.

J. H. Ruebush.

1. Come thou fount of ev'ry blessing, Tune my heart to sing Thy grace, (Thy grace,)
2. Jesus sought me when a stranger, Wand'ring from the fold of God, (of God,)
3. Prone to wander, Lord, I feel it, Prone to leave the God I love, (I love,)

Streams of mer-cy nev-er ceas-ing, Call for songs of loud-est praise.
He to res-cue me from dan-ger, In-terposed His precious blood.
Here's my heart, oh take and seal it, Seal it for Thy courts a-bove.

Refrain.

Oh the fount - ain flow-ing free - ly, All the
Oh the fountain ev - er flow-ing, flowing free for one and all, All the

thirst-y souls to heal, Free to all who will re-
thirst-y souls to heal, souls to heal, Free to all who will receive it, free to

ceive it, Come to Je-sus now and live.
all who will but ask,

Copyright, 1896, by The Ruebush-Kieffer Co.

No. 236. **God Will Help Thee.**

"God, even our Father, comfort your hearts.—2 THESS 2 : 16, 17."

Ida L. Reed. J. H. Hall.

1. What-so-ev-er be thy grief, God will help thee to en-dure,
2. God will help thee ev-er-more, If thou trust-ing lift thine eyes,
3. Let this prom-ise cheer thy heart, He will help and com-fort thee,
4. God will help thee day by day, We can nev-er-more for-get,

On-ly trust Him and be-lieve, All His prom-is-es are sure.
He will bear thee safe-ly o'er, All that here thy spir-it tries.
Nev-er let thy hope de-part, Ev-er-more thy friend will be.
Though the shad-ows cloud thy way, He will guard and guide thee yet.

Chorus.

He will help thee, He will help thee, Yield to Him and nev-er fear;

Give Him all thy doubts and troubles, He will all thy pleadings bear.

Copyright, 1896, by J. H. Hall.

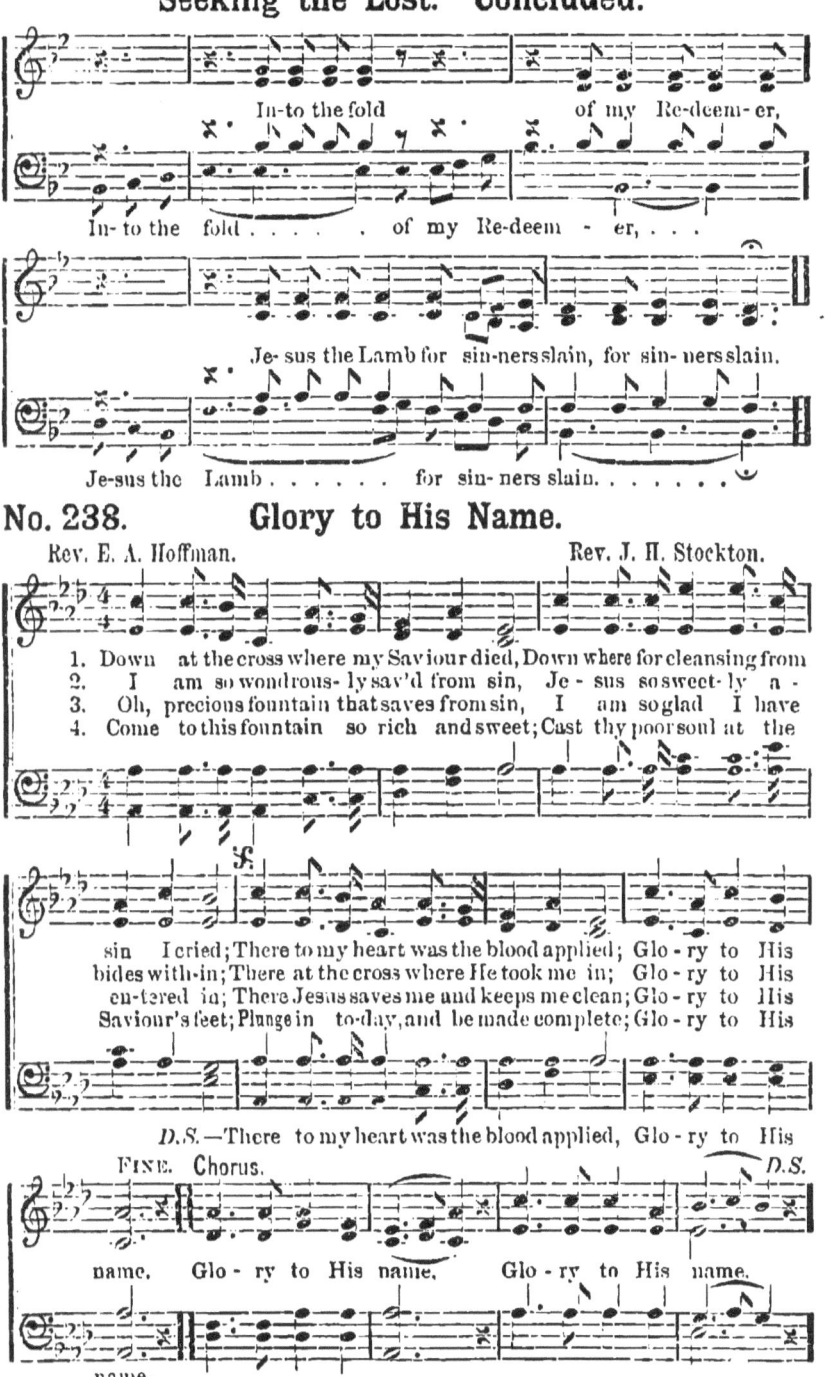

Wherever He Leads Me. Concluded.

shad-ows are past Then go home re-joic-ing to glo-ry, at last.

No. 240. A Song is in My Heart.

Mrs. Harriet E. Jones.   Geo. F. Rosche.

1. A song is in my heart to-day, For all my sins are wash'd a-way;
2. O sweet the song I've learned to sing In praise of my Re-deem-er, King;
3. O glad new song so full of joy, O song that shall my tongue employ

The precious blood has been applied, The blood of Christ, the Cru-ci-fied.
The song to par-don sin-ners dear, The song the an-gels love to hear.
Till called to join the blood-washed throng In that bright home of endless song.

Chorus.

O song of love, O song sublime, I feel like sing-ing all the time;

O song with-in my heart of hearts Since Christ my Lord His grace imparts.

Copyright, 1895, by Geo. F. Rosche, by per. All rights reserved.

No. 241.   "'Tis I! be not Afraid."

Anon.   W. A. Ogden.

1. Tho' toss'd with winds, and faint with fears, A - bove the tempest wild and drear,
2. These raging winds, this surging sea, Bear not a breath of wrath to thee;
3. 'Tis I who washed, and made thee white, 'Tis I who gave thy blind eyes sight,
4. When on the oth - er side, thy feet Shall stand midst thousand welcomes sweet,

Hark! hark! my Saviour's voice I hear, "'Tis I, be not a - fraid."
That storm has all been spent on me, "'Tis I, be not a - fraid."
'Tis I thy Lord, thy Life, thy Light, "'Tis I, be not a - fraid."
One well known voice thy heart shall greet, "'Tis I, be not a - fraid."

Chorus.

"'Tis I, be not a - fraid," "'Tis I, be not a - fraid,"
    "be not a-fraid,"   "be not afraid."

Hark! hark! my Saviour's voice I hear, "'Tis I, be not a - fraid."

Copyright, 1896, by The Buebush-Kieffer Co.

No. 249. **Oh! Why Not To-Night.**

"Come unto me, all ye that labor and are heavy laden and I will give you rest."—MATT. 11: 28.

Rev. H. Bonar, D. D.   J. Calvin Bushey.

1. Oh, do not let the word de-part, And close thine eyes against the light, Poor sin-ner, hard-en not your heart, Be saved, oh, to-night.
2. To-mor-row's sun may nev-er rise, To bless thy long de-lud-ed sight; This is the time, oh, then be wise, Be saved, oh, to-night.
3. Our Lord in pit-y lin-gers still, And wilt thou thus His love re-quite; Re-nounce at once thy stub-born will, Be saved, oh, to-night.
5. Our bless-ed Lord re-fus-es none, Who would to Him their souls u-nite, Be-lieve, o-bey, the work is done, Be saved, oh, to-night.

Chorus.

Oh, why not to-night? Oh, why not to-night? Wilt thou be saved? Then why not to-night?
Oh, why not to-night! why not to-night? why not to-night? Wilt thou be saved, wilt thou be saved, Then why not, oh, why not to-night?

Reentered and Copyright, 1895, by J. H. Hall.

No. 253. Greenville.

J. J. Rossseau.

1. { Come, Thou fount of ev-'ry blessing, Tune my heart to sing Thy grace;
   Streams of mer-cy nev-er ceas-ing, Call for songs of loud-est praise. }
2. { Here I'll raise mine Eb-en-e-zer, Hith-er by Thy help I'll come;
   And I hope, by thy good pleasure, Safe-ly to ar-rive at home. }

D.C.—Praise the Mount I'm fixed upon it, Mount of Thy re-deem-ing love.
D.C.— He, to res-cue me from danger, In-ter-posed His pre-cious blood.

Teach me some me-lo-dious son-net, Sung by flaming tongues above;
Je-sus sought me, when a stranger, Wand'ring from the fold of God;

No. 254. To Them that Love the Lord.

Rev. Geo. P. Hott. J. H. Hall.

1. To them that love the Lord, The prom-i-ses are giv'n.
2. To them that love the Lord, A few more sor-rows here,
3. To them that love the Lord, The saints se-cure-ly blest,

A hun-dred fold re-ward on earth, E-ter-nal life in heav'n.
A few more days of toil on earth, And Christ will then appear.
A life in Je-sus hid be-low, In heav'n e-ter-nal rest.

The Ruebush-Kieffer Co., owners of copyright.

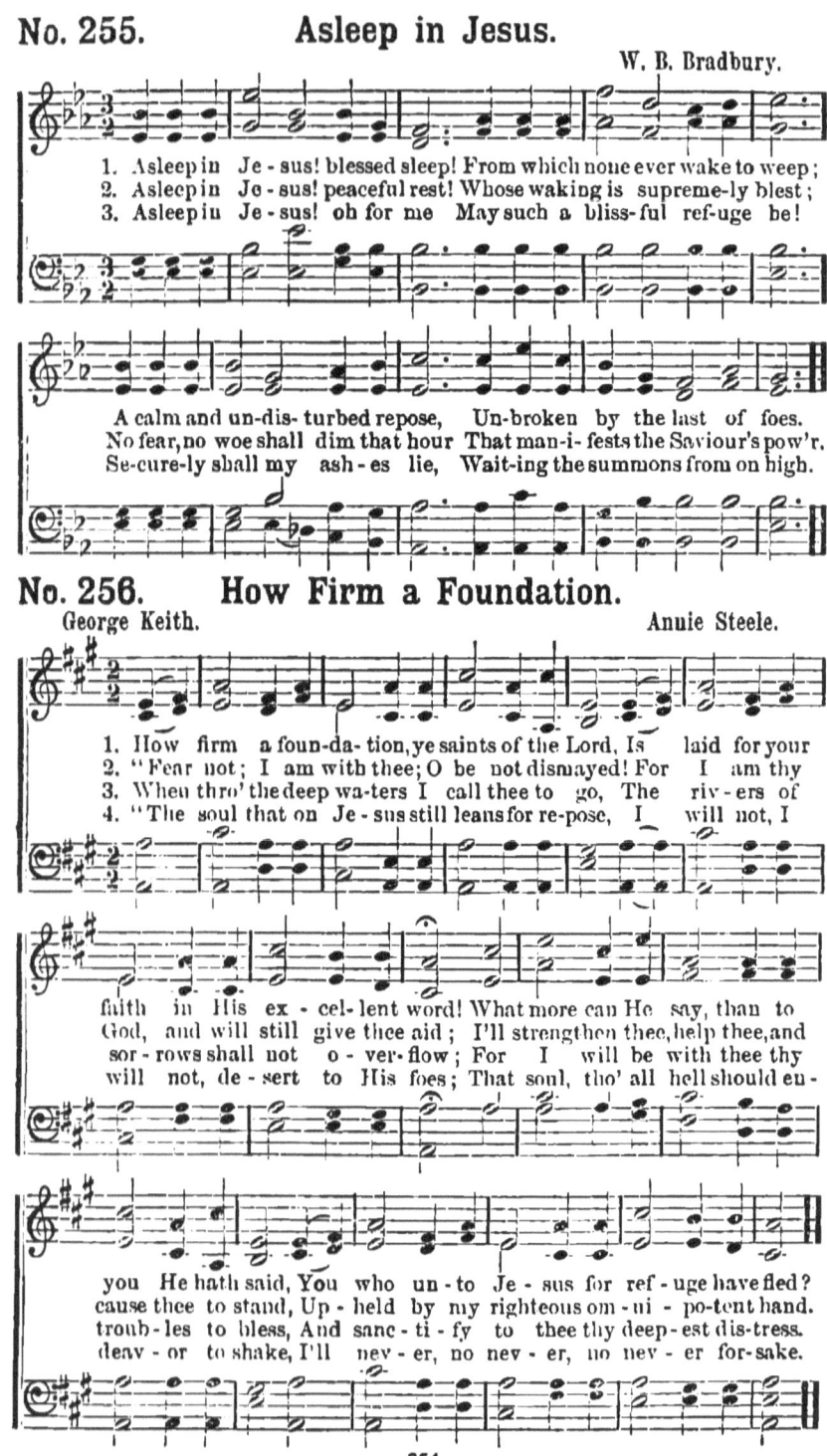

INDEX.

Title	NO.
Abide With Me	212
A Few More Years	141
America	257
A Song is in My Heart	240
Asleep in Jesus	255
At the Cross	139
A Work for All	199
Beneath His Wing	186
Benediction	258
Blessed Assurance	187
Boyleston	252
Bright Canaan	211
By the Crystal Sea	188
Calling Me Over the Tide	157
Christian Battle Cry	180
Christ or the World	213
Christ is All	215
Clinging to Jesus Alone	227
Come Ye that Love the Lord	152
Come Back, Wanderer	171
Come, Sinner, Come	194
Crown After Cross	131
Dear Lord, Remember Me	202
Death is Only a Dream	203
Don't You Want to be Ready?	149
Fair Haven	222
Follow Him	158
Footsteps of Jesus	192
Friend Unfailing	208
Glad Tidings of Joy	138
Glory Over There	167
Glory to His Name	238
God Calling Yet	217
God Will Help Thee	236
Gratitude	224
Greenville	253
Guide Me, Saviour	201
Hallelujah, Bless His Name	196
Hark! the Saviour Calls	172
Heaven is Not Far Away	206
He Came to Save Me	246
Ho! Every One That Thirsteth	161
Home of the Soul	181
How Firm a Foundation	256
I Love to Tell the Story	197
In Sight of the Crystal Sea	209
Is My Name Written There?	216
I Want to Live for Jesus	185
Jesus is Calling	190
Jesus, Saviour, Pilot Me	210
Jesus Will Save	134
Jesus Will Let You In	226
Joy to the World	136
Land of Promise	154
Lead Me Only Home, Father	169
Lead Me to the Rock	193
Little Ones Like Me	191
March On	229
Marching Orders	144
My Faith Looks Up to Thee	150
My Church, My Dear Old Church	164

Title	NO.
O for a Faith	251
Oh! I am so Happy	179
On the Wings of Morn	159
Onward to the Fray	175
O! Prodigal, Don't Stay Away	219
O! Why Not To-Night?	249
Our Nation for Jesus	145
Passing This Way	143
Redeeming Love	148
Rest in the Lord	156
Save Me Now	184
Saviour, Guide Me	242
Seeking a Refuge	165
Seeking for Me	189
Seeking the Lost	237
Send the Glad Tidings	137
Shall I Let Him In?	182
Sinner, Won't You Come to Jesus?	177
Sing Glory	214
Softly and Tenderly	147
Sowing the Tares	198
Speak, O Lord	247
Stand Up for Jesus	178
Standing on the Promises	205
Step in the Life-boat	195
Strive to Follow Jesus	221
Tell Me All About Jesus	183
Tell it to Jesus	207
The Blessing of Song	135
The Beautiful Golden Gate	200
The Flowing Water	163
The Faithful Pilot	173
The Flowing Fountain	234
The Great Physician	232
The Happy Day	162
The Loving Little Ones	228
The One Whom Jesus Loved	244
The Open Fountain	218
The Star of Bethlehem	133
The Story Sweet and Old	140
The Song I Love	146
The Stranger at the Door	170
The Story Tell Again	233
There's a Mighty Army Marching	142
The Wondrous Cross	223
'Tis I, be Not Afraid	241
To Them That Love the Lord	254
Trusting in the Love of Jesus	176
Trust in the Lord	220
Turning to God	204
Victory O'er the Grave	151
Waiting at the Pool	248
Walking in the King's Highway	245
We are Marching on	153
We are Pilgrims of a Day	235
We Come, Come Again	160
We'll Never Say Good-Bye	250
Weeping One of Bethany	230
What are You Recording?	142
What Shall Our Answers Be?	231
Wherever He Leads Me	239
When the King Comes in	243
When Thou Comest	166
Where the Living Water Flows	225
Will You Come to the Feast	174
Ye are My Witnesses	168
Yield Not to Temptation	155

www.ingramcontent.com/pod-product-compliance
Lightning Source LLC
Chambersburg PA
CBHW020111170426
43199CB00009B/488